Toriana

CATHERINE BEZOLD

DEDICATION

To my family and friends who have weathered the storms
with me in prayer and love

CONTENTS

ACKNOWLEDGMENTS

I would like to acknowledge my editors Janine Ayrton, Heidi Short and Judy Braune. I am also grateful for Dr Robert Falconer who designed my book cover.

1 CATHERINE

For You are my hope, O Lord God you are my trust from my youth.
By You I have been upheld from birth. You are He who took me out
of my mother's womb. My praise shall be continually of You.

Psalm 71:5-6 (NKJV)

My heart was racing and I knew Jesus wanted me to share something that I had read from the Bible in the last week. Every Sunday I came to church with my parents and brother. It was the common practice of this congregational church that men would come prepared with a Bible passage that they felt the church needed to hear. In the first part of the service all children remained with their family and later went to Sunday school. I was only 9 years old, and I could still hear my heart pounding as I contemplated standing up and reading before the congregation. What would these big people think of me? I had seen men stand up and preach and sometimes women but not someone small like me. I remembered something they once talked about in Sunday school, that we shouldn't fear man but God. So with my Bible in hand I stood up. My hand was shaking as I flipped the thin pages of my Bible and started to read. As I recited the verses, I realised that it is the Lord who gives us the boldness to speak when He wants to use us to impact someone's life. My hope was that God's Words would challenge people to put their hearts right before Him, before they had to die or Jesus returned. I felt a bit like the little boy offering his loaves and fishes. What mattered was his love and obedience to God. All that mattered to me was God and pleasing Him. He had been my constant companion throughout my childhood. I closed my Bible and sat down and my heart was galloping from my chest to my shaking hands. My mum squeezed my hand and I felt her affirmation, and God's peace that I had done the right thing. After the service one of the men encouraged me by saying that the words I spoke touched him. I remember feeling so happy and somehow I no longer felt any fear when it came to sharing something like that again. If only I had remained in childlike faith. If only our family had remained in His love and guidance.

My childhood was not an easy one. I can remember late one night looking through my little side bedroom window and seeing my mum and dad arguing. I loved them so much and hated them fighting. As a child you never understand the things of the adult world, you just want the people you love to love each other. I had made Jesus a part of my life and wept on my pillow, asking Him to please help them. At that moment it wasn't so much that they stopped, or that the problems went away but I felt the presence of Jesus carrying me through. My parents loved my brother and I very much but their marriage had fallen apart and ended in divorce. My father was a broken man; he had also lost his company, his family and his car. Broken he came to the front of his church and gave it all to God. The Lord met him, comforted him and gave him a promise that he would turn the hearts of the fathers to their children and the hearts of their children to their fathers. He prayed and believed and asked me in my early 20´s if he could have a second chance.

In life I realised it's never too late to begin anew and I admired my father for being real and not being afraid to start again. I gave him a second chance. He had been on a parenting course and I agreed to participate. In this day and age I think people thought I was crazy but I saw the recent decisions I had made in relationships had not been so wise.

At the age of 17 I'd fallen in love. It was a week of outings together with other schools. I had been in St Mary's Girls School for 5 years and was excited to interact with young people from different walks of life. I was travelling with a group of students to an English workshop. We stopped and I stood up to leave but my eyes met with the eyes of a young man on the same bus. I felt as if he could see straight into my heart. My cheeks grew warm as I quickly looked away. He just happened to be going to the same cultural talk and I was pleasantly surprised to see that he sat next to me. At first I tried to concentrate on what was being said by the main speaker. But I couldn't with this wonderful man sitting next to me. In the break we remained glued to our chairs and started sharing different things about our lives and it was just incredible. We exchanged our telephone numbers and spent the next couple of days speaking for at least an hour. I had never met a man that could listen and talk so much on the phone. He was so kind and gentle. Our first dance at our school social, our first kiss before a beautiful sunset and many moments of smiles and laughter were all my dreams coming true! He continually told me how my eyes captured him from the first moment we met and that he loved looking at them. My whole world began to revolve around him. We ended up going to the same university in Cape Town and everything seemed to be going so well. Then God brought some good Christian friends across my path. They tried many a time to share with me that a Christian and a non-Christian are two worlds that cannot mix. But I was blind and in love. I had been together with him for just over two years and was planning to marry him. However my nights became restless and I could not sleep as I began to realise that I had to choose between this man or God. I became so convicted that if I really loved this man I could not live a lie anymore and wrote him a note that I needed to see him urgently. I waited in my university residence for him to come. How do you begin to tell someone you love so much that it is not meant to be? As I tried to put the words together his first response was absolute shock. He felt we could get married despite our different beliefs. I told him if we had children I would want them to join me in learning about Jesus. Because he was an atheist he felt my views should not be imposed on our children. Our eyes met but this time with tears and there was a wall between us. We knew it wouldn't work. As he left, my heart felt torn.

It took over a year for my heart to heal, but I was comforted by our Lord that I had made the right decision. I was 20 and enrolled at our church camp. Rockland's was at a beautiful place on the coast and it was a special time of healing for me. After one of the talks I went forward for prayer and was unaware that a young man was watching and praying for me. He offered to take me home after the camp and he was kind. This was the start of my second relationship now with a Christian man. Our first intentions were pure and for marriage. I realised that he had become my rescuer, someone to replace the love I had lost and help me through my parents' divorce. But it should have been Jesus that I ran to and not man. Just because he was a

Christian didn't mean that he was part of God's divine plan for me. After two years we parted ways, it was painful and I felt desperately lonely. It was in this moment that my father came and asked for a second chance. It meant sharing my dreams with him, telling him if and when, I had feelings for someone, it meant being totally open and submitting to his leadership. It was in this time that I returned to the dreams I had when I was younger.

My dream since I was a young girl was to be a missionary. I was in awe of any stories that I was told of various missionaries and each story was a seed that slowly grew this dream. I loved reading the Bible even when I didn't fully understand it, and what I read I believed. I wanted to follow Jesus and totally believed He was real. I loved Him deeply. At the age of 14 my desire was to be obedient to God's Word and in love I chose to be baptised. It was a public testimony, a symbol of His death and resurrection and that Jesus was my Lord.

Those days were the "good" times, when I felt close to God, and I wanted that closeness again… that childlike faith, that passion to serve and follow Christ. I had lost that closeness as I put a man in the centre of my world, but now I wanted to pick up my childhood dreams again and put Jesus in the centre of my life. This decision my father fully supported, praying with me and helping me find direction. It was like being in the nest, being under my father's wings growing from an eaglet into an eagle, getting ready to fly. He and my step-mum gave me a plain silver ring for my birthday. Inside was engraved "Catherine woman of God." It was significant for me as I had never felt fully secure in myself. But in God I could begin to stand tall, begin to see myself as someone beautiful, not in men's sight but in God's.

Embarking on a dream to become a life time missionary takes much prayer and time of practical preparation in one's home church. My mentor Janine and my pastors guided me in these steps. My father too had prayed and guided me and felt it was time to let me go. So one day he had two white doves in a box and asked me to come into the garden. I held the one bird and my father the other. We stood, my eyes welling up with tears, feeling the softness of this beautiful dove between my fingers, we prayed and dad gave his father's blessing. At the end of the blessing, we let the birds flutter into the freedom of the blue sky. This was it. We had grown so close and now we had to let go, like Abraham putting Isaac on the altar. This was my father's symbol of me leaving his nest and letting me go.

2 RABBIT

Be strong and of good courage do not be afraid, do not be dismayed,
for the Lord your God is with you wherever you go.

Joshua 1:9

Looking out of the plane window - the airport, my family and friends, Table Mountain and the sea - once such a large part of my life were now becoming smaller. In my hand I clutched some cards, the words bringing love and comfort, and encouragement to be strong and courageous. Here I was alone in the plane leaving everything, everyone I loved and held so dear. I realized at that moment how easy it is to be strong and courageous when surrounded by friends and family. At the airport my grandfather had held me so tight and said: "You won't see me again." I loved him so much. I told him that of course I would see him again when I came back for holidays.

I seemed so sure that everyone would remain just as they were when I left them. This was my dream to leave all that I held dear for the sake of the call, the call to follow Jesus Christ as a missionary. Evangelizing and walking alongside a group of people, teaching and guiding them on better pathways of life was what I wanted to do. My desire was to help them grow in a relationship with Jesus. I was overwhelmed, scared and excited. I stepped out in faith knowing that His plans were to prosper me and not to harm me. I was travelling this dream alone. I was single.

The first part of this dream began on a missionary ship, when I was standing in a crowded dining room. It was filled with chatter and the aroma of different varieties of food. Even the cry of the seagulls, with the lapping of the sea against the barge could be heard through the open portholes. My tray accompanied with a small plate of pasta and a cup of steamy hot tea and I had a feeling of uncertainty of where to place myself. I could sit at the empty table or I could be strong and courageous and sit with new people. I can remember how I was drawn to the table where people were laughing the most, and I recognized a South African accent. So I took the plunge and began a wonderful journey of getting to know new people. I learnt the importance of being open and friendly even when you don't feel like it and adding a little smile and a touch of humor. It also helped me to be a good listener as I saw how many people longed to share their hearts and not just their daily life. I lived in a tiny cabin with three roommates, two Americans and one Belgian. In my family I was nicknamed the "Rabbit"! Whenever I arrived for a visit I would first go to my room, unpack everything, put up some photos and pictures that were familiar and then I felt at home. I was then ready to come out of my "burrow" and be with my family. So, true to habit, my first few hours on the ship were spent in my cabin, getting my bunk, a shelf, a few drawers and a cupboard to look more "like home". Only once I was settled was I ready to begin preparing myself for the new task that lay ahead. My ministry was to be a primary school teacher on board for the children of those who were ministering elsewhere on the ship, as doctors, chefs, accountants, engineers and more.

The desire to be a teacher on board this Christian ship evolved over a number of years. When I completed secondary schooling I had decided to study Human Resource Management at the University of Cape Town. I loved working with people and felt this profession would be a good learning experience in my life. Once I had successfully completed this three year degree I was led to join a company as their Human Resource manager. It was a learning curve and I definitely learnt professionalism and the stresses involved in being part of the corporate world. On weekends I enjoyed working with my church in the slum areas of Cape Town helping with Sunday school. My love for children grew in this time and my desire to work with them, specifically in a mission context, became my overwhelming dream. I then returned to UCT to study a Higher Diploma in Primary School Education. This journey had led me to where I was now standing in my new cabin classroom preparing exciting lessons. I had a desire not only to teach them what they needed to learn but to love them and create a joyful environment where they too could discover Jesus in a new and dynamic way. I had a wonderful principal and team of staff that were incredibly supportive of my ideas.

Life serving on the ship at times was beautiful and other times frightening. Some days were beautiful and calm, an expanse of blue skies with no end, with the occasional visit of a school of dolphins who surfed the wake of the ship's bow. Other days were making sure everything in our cabin and classroom was tied down and secure. Keeping myself steady on the corridor walls or trying to focus on teaching a Math's lesson when all I felt like doing was being sick! One particular rough day while we had school break with the children playing on the deck, suddenly a huge wave hit the side and deck of the ship! We were wet through and shocked and came into the safety of the classroom. The bookshelf had been knocked half way across the classroom by the wave and all the books had been flung onto the floor. The ropes used to tie everything down were not strong enough for that big wave!

I sometimes felt like that too, that I was not able to tie down the feelings going around in my heart and mind. There were days filled with deep meaningful conversations with the children about God and Jesus. Early 5am prayer meetings with good friends and times with my new friends were full of fun, laughter and joy! Life seemed calm and good. But then came the wave of loneliness as some of my new-found friends' term on the ship was over and they were going home. In my heart I just wanted to be strong and courageous, keep all things together and in control. I wanted to keep things all nicely tied up. Living together in a small cabin, not having space or place to work through my thoughts was hard. The "big wave" that hit my life at that time was the phone call from my father telling me that my grandfather had passed away. At that time I realized I didn't have everything in control. Feeling absolutely numb, my mind drifted to a few months before when he had phoned me for Christmas. I missed him and my family so much that all I could do was weep on the phone...all I could manage to say was how much I loved him. When I was leaving the ship to attend the funeral, my beloved class of children huddled around me and one of the precious boys cried as he thought I would never come back. He put his arm around me and said: "Miss Fitzpatrick, please don't leave me, please promise me you will come back." I promised him I would as I flew back home to mourn with my family.

Nothing was the same from when I had left home. However Grandpa's clothes and slippers were still where he had left them before going to play golf. I held my dearest granny Doreen as we cried and she said she couldn´t move the slippers as she felt like grandpa would come home any moment. But we both knew that he wouldn´t. Friends had moved on in their own lives, some married, some with children – they were still there for me but it felt different. I realized that this is the reality of life. Things do change, people change, people grow old, people die, circumstances change but Jesus never changes. He is the same yesterday, today and tomorrow. Jesus said, "Whoever desires to come after me, let him deny himself, take up his cross and follow me"(NKJV Mark 8v34). We all have our crosses to bear but what I realized is that he said "follow me," not walk alone but come with me! He didn´t say be strong and courageous and walk this narrow path alone. He said be not afraid for I the Lord am with you wherever you go (NKJV Joshua 1v9). So I returned to the ship as I promised the little boy in my class and continued with the plans God had for me. Yes I was single but not alone.

3 CATI

The Lord is near to those who have a broken heart, and saves such as have a contrite Spirit.

Psalm 34:18

The morning was filled with a piercing scream and it came from the valley below. There was not just one scream but many. Freetown was under attack. It was all so sudden. Where to run to? They seemed so evil and nobody knew where they had all come from. Many could only cry out "Oh God!" The presenter on the radio prayed "Jesus help us" and many listeners seemed to echo this cry. A pregnant woman was harassed and asked if she was having a boy or a girl? In West Africa the medical equipment required to answer this kind of question is not available. So the mother-to-be had no answer…and the machete held by the interrogator sliced her open. He found his answer and then left her and her unborn child to die. Others lost their arms or legs. Families were torn apart, there was no time to say goodbye, just run! In many cases the forest was a safer option. Today the nightmare lives on.

This is not my story but the story of my beloved brothers and sisters in Freetown, Sierra Leone. Our ship came with the hope and love of Jesus to help them rebuild their lives. My relationship with these wonderful people began over a meal. I had come with my friends from the ship to their church service up on the hill, overlooking

Freetown. It was an honor for them to have us join them, as my ship friends had helped design and build their little clinic. The ship had various ministries and one of them was a building team. My cabin mate was the architect on the team. She invited me to join them as the church had invited them all to a special service. At the end of the service our brothers and sisters came towards us with large plates of food. I saw little children hiding behind a nearby mound with big wide eyes looking as if roast chicken and chips had just passed them by. Outwardly I had a huge smile of thanks as the plate was put before me but inwardly I didn't know if I would be able to stomach this meal. It was their very best offering of "Cassava" leaves mixed with whole fish, eyes and all. As a missionary I learnt that it is an insult not to eat the food offered and prayed for God to help me. Then I had an idea…I asked the elders of the church if they had some extra spoons as I would like the children to join me in eating this wonderful meal. To my delight they quickly brought some spoons and I welcomed the children around my plate. I took the first mouthful and ate very slowly and the children with great excitement ate most of the food by the time I tried the second mouthful. Thank you Lord! This was the beginning of a very special relationship with these wonderful children. Long after the food was finished they were playing with my hair and we were just enjoying each others' company.

During the week, I had been doing a bible study with a group of ladies on the ship called "Experiencing God"[1], and we had just learnt about joining God where He is already working. I had prayed that God would show me where He was working so I could join Him. Little did I know that my prayer would be answered so quickly. The elders of this little church on the hill had been praying for God to provide them with someone to help start a Sunday

---

[1] Blackaby H. 2005. *Experiencing God.* Lifeway:Nashville.

school. So they saw me and asked if I would embrace this challenge. I prayed about it and saw it as joining God where He was already working and it began a fantastic new ministry.

I asked the church to provide me with four women to disciple. This they did with great excitement, and with the anticipation of a new Sunday school. These ladies had such beautiful hearts and joined me as we began. As I worked alongside them I saw that God had given them incredible gifts to teach and felt that this ministry could grow into more than a simple Sunday school but a Christian primary school too! I shared these ideas with the church and was greatly surprised to see how they embraced my dreams for the school. I was able to help them to start at a teachers training college but they together with God's help had to complete this journey without me. We had been in Freetown for six months. The ships main ministry was medical work and outreach. The medical teams had completed their surgeries, patients had recovered and returned home. So, we as a crew started preparing to leave for our next port of call. I felt I had just begun my work and was very sad to leave my new-found friends and ministry. Just before I left a little baby girl was born to one of the church members and they named her "Cati" after me; it was very special to be able to hold her and pray for her before our ship left.

As we sailed away and they grew smaller and smaller standing at the harbor, in my heart my love for them grew bigger and bigger and I hoped that God would one day bring me back to them. I also realized that I was called to disciple the nations and wanted more than going from port to port with seeds for evangelism. This thought remained in my heart and prayers as I continued the task before me serving as a teacher onboard the ship.

4 MISS FITZPATRICK

When the Lord saw her, he felt compassion for her. He said to her, "You can stop crying.

Luke 7:13

"Miss Fitzpatrick, Miss Fitzpatrick, come quickly!" cried one of my students on the ship. I dropped the books on my desk and followed my students to one corner of the deck, and there we saw the most beautiful thing. Thousands upon thousands of butterflies were migrating across the sea and our ship was right in the center of this migration. We stood there in awe and put our hands out to give the butterflies a chance to rest. It was wonderful to see the delight on my students' faces as the tiny creatures landed on their fingers. It was like being in another world, God's world. Some landed in my hair and they tickled my ears, but I didn't mind. These beautiful creatures gently touching us, the smell of the salty sea and the sound of the waves against the bow of our ship, made it an experience we would all never forget. It felt as though we were in a whirlwind of beauty.

Most of my days were spent in the classroom, with ten little disciples in my class, each with their own characters and personalities. I enjoyed getting to know each of them and especially liked to discover how I could inspire them in their talents and gifts. Whether we were at sea together or docked at a port our lessons were always an adventure.

During this time we came to be at port in Gambia and on weekends I missed my Sierra Leone friends and longed to be with them again. In my heart I didn't want to start looking for another ministry in our new port in Ghana. I seemed to get attached to the people God led me to and was afraid to start that journey again. Some friends on the ship encouraged me to get involved in visiting the children's ward of the Ghana hospital. To be honest the thought of a hospital makes me feel faint. The smell of the disinfectant seems to run from my nostrils and through my entire body. The sight of any patient with blood would cause a sudden dizziness and I need to look away. In my journey with the Lord, often when I would say "No God, I can't do this", I would find Him leading me into the things I feared the most. I prayed in anguish about it but knew that God wanted me to go. Somehow I felt He wanted to teach me something about Himself through this experience.

Early one Saturday morning I joined the team. On the way our nurse explained that we were assigned to the burn unit of the children's ward. As we opened the door we could hear the agonizing screams of the children down the corridor. I was so afraid that I would not be able to handle the situation. As we stepped into the ward I saw feeble little bodies writhing on their beds in agony. Somehow the Holy Spirit took over and my whole being was overwhelmed with compassion. I tried to find a part on one particular precious little child's body that was not burned and began to pray like I had never prayed before.

I saw a thin young boy sitting in an awkward position on his bed. At first I was relieved that his body did not look burnt and started to play with him. His fingers were too weak to play, so together with both our hands we managed. Some of the doctors and nurses came towards his bed to examine him and change dressings. They slowly removed the blankets covering his legs and he started to writhe in anticipation of the pain. I kept my arms around him to comfort him. He knew the agony that lay ahead and I was soon to see and understand. As the bandages were slowly peeled away I saw white open raw flesh. They began cleansing and disinfecting and he squeezed my hand as hard as he could and I held his hand in mine, praying with tears in my eyes for God's miraculous healing.

In the opposite bed lay a little girl and most of her body was covered in bandages. As the doctors approached her bed she started screaming. I asked the nurse if they had any medicine for pain or to calm her but they said they had run short of supplies and proceeded as carefully as they could. My ship colleague called me over to help hold the little girl down. I tried to find a part of her body that was not burnt and as I touched and held her I asked Jesus please to remove all pain and fear and that the Holy Spirit would calm her and heal her. Once all the dressings had been changed we began our program. As a team we decided to sing songs, act like clowns, play with balloons and tell Jesus stories. We did everything that we could to keep their minds off the pain. It was really incredible to see their eyes light up with joy and to hear the ward filled with laughter instead of screaming. It was hard to leave them and I spent much of the week praying scripture over their lives and bodies and hoped to see God's restoration the following Saturday.

When we arrived the next Saturday, I was surprised when we opened the door of the clinic that there were no echoing screams coming down the corridor. Most of the children were now sitting up in their beds and we were enchanted by their faces that lit up with joy at the sight of us. The most incredible miracle for me was the little girl who had been burnt all over her body. The nurses were busy changing her dressing and she sat smiling. As I looked at her wounds I saw that they had healed significantly. Our eyes met and she grinned at me with the biggest smile. It was if we both knew in that instant that Jesus in his mercy and compassion was healing her. Each week we came we shared bible stories and some children committed their lives to Jesus. I watched as Jesus changed faces of pain to faces of joy. I began to understand His heart and compassion for the sick and praised Him for this incredible opportunity I had of seeing His healing touch.

5 MISS FITZ

He who says He abides in Him, ought himself also to walk just as
He walked.

1 John 2:6

I believe with all my heart that God's Word does not
return void, but I also feel an overwhelming sense that we
are called to walk alongside a people group, teaching and
guiding them on better pathways of life, helping them to
grow in a relationship with our Lord and discipling people
as Jesus did. The ship had been a great learning curve for
me but it was time to move to the next stepping stone of
my life. I wanted to develop more in the area of working
among a people group for a longer period of time.

At this time came the great opportunity to join a sister
church of my church in Cape Town, South Africa, helping
develop a Christian Primary School in the Khayelitsha
township. Nelson Mandela once said that if you speak to a
person you can capture his mind but if you speak his
mother tongue you capture his heart. Learning not only a
language but a culture became crucial to working with my
brothers and sisters in the townships. It took more than
being a teacher and helping establish a school, but
speaking their language, understanding their hearts and
what they had been through in the apartheid years. I was
born in South Africa and was only a young girl during the
intense and violent years of apartheid. I didn't really know

or understand what was happening in my own country. I happened to have a white face that placed me in a better position at the time and had no concept of what they went through. I decided to invite the pastor of the church to share with my grade 3 History Class about his experience in those years. My grandmother always told me how important it was to learn history. The hope was that it could influence our minds in such a way that we would try our utmost not to allow history to repeat itself. The pastor told of his dreadful experiences during the 1980's and 90's of how he was part of a political party to help his people fight for freedom. Freedom to vote, freedom to live in their own country, freedom to choose the education they wanted for their children, freedom to sit on any beach and freedom to sit on a bench even if it was labeled for whites only! He completed his story and left the classroom. I remember my little pupils sitting there dumbstruck with their braided hair and dark brown eyes full of questions. "Miss, he is not telling the truth is he?" "Did you sit on a white's only bench?" I stood before them ashamed just nodding my head. They had such love for me a white woman that they wouldn't even believe a story from their own pastor, their own kind.

Somehow it also brought me hope that in this new generation of children there would be no memories of being separate, but only new memories of being part of a colorful "rainbow nation" full of freedom!

Looking back, I can remember my last year of school in 1994, our first democratic elections. So many people prayed as we expected violence. But God in his mercy granted us peace. He gave our leaders wisdom and Nelson Mandela did not fight for revenge but thought of future generations. He desired to build a foundation of freedom and hope and not one of bloodshed. I admired and respected him and am grateful that I had the opportunity to work amongst my people planting seeds that would grow these children into wonderful men and women that would be proud to be a part of their country.

During my years serving in Khayelitsha townships, my mind often drifted to my dear friends in Sierra Leone. Our School holidays were in a few months time. I prayed with my mentor Janine and we decided this would be a good open window to return to Sierra Leone for a visit. We wrote letters and emails. God provided a VISA for Sierra Leone via London and I was ready to go! My suitcase was full of resources for the school. For myself I simply had a sleeping bag, a mosquito net, a dress or two and some toiletries. My flights were interesting and the landing a bit bumpy but it was all worth it as I saw the faces of my wonderful friends. We had to sail from the airport via ferry to get to Freetown. Oh, it was so wonderful to be back, climbing up the familiar hill and reuniting with little "Cati." It was beautiful and emotional all at once. On this journey I decided to live amongst the people. It was an incredible eye opener.

Early one morning we carried our clothes to the river and together washed ourselves and our clothes. Somehow a dark African woman blends more into her surroundings than a pale skinned woman like me! A large cup of tea was our breakfast and the day began. It was thrilling to see how the church had planned and built a primary school a joining the church. I had only planted the seeds about a primary school, the church community had watered it but God had made it grow. One of the teachers that I had trained rang the brass school bell and all the children stood in straight lines, smartly dressed in their school uniforms. They had been sown by one of the teachers. Another teacher had "Cassava" root snacks for the children at tea time break. My heart was filled with joy as I looked at the classrooms and the desks and saw a place of safety and learning for these precious little ones.

Each day I spent with them I leant more about their experiences during the rebel war. At first they didn't want to talk about it, they wanted to blot it out of their memories. One afternoon a woman wanted to braid my long hair. As we sat on the front patio, her fingers gliding through my hair, she just started sharing what had happened to her. One by one different people came and added to her story. I shared with them how healing can only come when we share what we experienced and bring it before God. We then decided together with the church leaders to make a prayer walk around the entire area of their town. As we walked and prayed we asked Jesus for His grace and forgiveness, for Him to wash away the bloodstains of their lost family members, to heal the broken-hearted and to help the community grow in their relationship with Jesus. It was incredible for me to watch God move in the contrite hearts of these beautiful people. He heard their cry, came near to them and I saw God begin the process of healing in them.

Early the next morning I found a beautiful African outfit that my friends had made for me. It was Sunday and I had been asked to preach the message. The church was full and as I shared God's Word, the scripture from Isaiah 61:1 came to my mind. "The Spirit of the Lord God is upon me, because the Lord has anointed me to preach good tidings to the poor and has sent me to heal the broken-hearted." It was a privilege to follow in the footprints of Jesus in Sierra Leone. Eventually the day came for me to leave and it was hard. I had been there for a season and I could see the church, Sunday School and Primary School had become a light on a hill that could not be hidden away.

This journey to Sierra Leone had again sparked my passion to go to the nations and people-groups that were unreached and needed Jesus. Each holiday break I had from school I used to join my church on mission trips.

6 GENERAL FITZ

Therefore we also, since we are surrounded by so great a cloud of witnesses, let us lay aside every weight, and the sin that so easily ensnares us, and let us run with endurance the race that is set before us.

Hebrews 12:1

As the glow of the setting sun was swallowed by the Zambezi River, many different kinds of animals cautiously made their way down to the water to take a final drink before it became completely dark. With each paddle stroke my muscles were aching. We had been rowing for hours and would only stop when the tide changed. Inspired by God and David Livingstone we felt called to the tribes along the Zambezi River that had never heard about Jesus. With one passion and one heart we kept rowing. We were a team of eight people from my home church in Cape Town and two local guides from Mozambique rowing two red inflatable boats. Our aim was to row up the Zambezi River, through a Zambezi Delta to a coastal region of Mozambique that had not been reached. The team was largely men, me and another young woman from our church. I was determined not to let the team down. I felt that, as a female, it was important to train at the gym to qualify for this four week mission over my school holidays. I had spent many hours at the gym; doing pushups and pull-ups, running, cycling and rowing, making sure that I was as physically ready for this trip as I could possibly be. Even though my muscles ached I kept rowing. The sun had set and the jungle seemed to be a mass of moving shadows. All you could hear was our breathing, together with the lapping of water at each stroke of our oars. Suddenly we heard from the boat ahead of us…"BACK! BACK! BACK!" It was pitch dark and they seemed far to the left of us. There was splashing, yelling and then grunting. In my heart I prayed, "Oh Lord protect them, whatever animal it is, You have power to overcome it." The splashing came closer and closer towards us. We were afraid to put our torches on in case it angered the animal even more. As the image drew near to us we saw the shapes and faces of our friends, ash white with shock. "We hit a hippo!" they exclaimed. I felt numb and wanted to cry, but the men in the team all just seemed shocked and excited and continued rowing through the night. So, putting on a brave face, I followed their lead and continued to paddle, praying with each paddle stroke that we would not hit a crocodile or hippo. It took all my emotional energy to carve my oar into the dark black water. When the tide eventually changed we stopped on the riverbank. Getting out of our boats, we stepped straight into thick, deep mud, and we made our way through the squelching mess to a reasonably flat part of riverbank. I had a tent to myself and the guys helped me set it up in the middle of the horse shoe-shaped arrangement of tents. The entire team was exhausted and everyone collapsed into their tents to try to get some sleep. I too was exhausted but couldn't bear to climb into my nice clean sleeping bag full of mud. So I took a couple of wet wipes and methodically cleaned my body and then managed to climb into my pajamas. I fell asleep as my head hit my make-shift pillow of clothes and socks.

Early the next morning, as I emerged from my tent, the guys were all shocked to see me clean and in my pajamas. As muddy as they were they had all just collapsed on top of their sleeping bags and gone to sleep. It made it easy for them in the morning as they were all ready to go as they stepped out of their tents. I, on the other hand, needed to get back into my "work" clothes and get ready for the day ahead. I discovered that it is somewhat challenging trying to change clothes in a tiny tent, knowing that there is a team of men waiting outside and chomping at the bit to get going with their day! But eventually I was ready and we started rowing upriver again.

Our third day of rowing was going to be a race against the tide. In the last couple of days we had been rowing in fairly large rivers. But the further we rowed up the Zambezi, and the closer we came to the ocean, the river started forming into little rivers called Deltas. The challenge facing our guides was to get us to the smallest of the deltas at the point at which the tide was its highest, allowing us enough opportunity, and water, to row through the Delta region to the coast where this tribe was situated. On this particular day, as we entered the Delta, it seemed to be at just the right level of water for our boats to pass through. However, our guide soon started to tell us to row faster as it seemed that the tide was running out. It happened so quickly, as though someone had pulled a plug from the bathtub. In minutes all the water was gone and in seconds we were stuck in the mud. But this was to become the least of our problems as, all of sudden, and quite unexpectedly, we were under attack by thousands upon thousands of mosquitos, all bombarding us like miniature "kamikaze" pilots. Our arms and faces were literally transformed into a mass of black, swarming insects, and, it appeared that the more we tried to hit at them and kill, the more they attacked us. Looking ahead of us, I saw the tracks left by crocodiles as they slid into the water, as well as traces of many other kinds of animals. Thankfully, our team leader chose that moment to revert back to the days he spent in the Army, announcing, "Gentlemen stopping is not an option! Fitz you go ahead of the boats and pull out all branches and broken trees to clear the way." Determined to embrace the challenge, I prayed in Jesus' name and charged ahead, diving into the mud and pulling out branches and things that could have caused a puncture in the boat. In my heart I had the fleeting thought that if I died at least it would be whilst doing the Lord's work! The men pushed our two boats filled with our water supplies, food and tents. It was like pushing a large animal through the mud. It felt like a war, we were covered in mud and mosquitos with the men pushing so hard that some of them were even vomiting. Finally, we saw water and it encouraged us to push faster until the boats glided and then eventually floated. With the strength of God we made it through to the other side. Our guide was fearing that we would be angry with him, but instead the team were all giving each other high fives and jumping for victory when we reached water and could row again. Within minutes, we were rowing again and the men were cracking jokes around me! All I wanted to do was burst into tears. I realized that men and women are very different, but somehow I thought that if I cried it would dampen their high spirits, so I held all my emotions in check.

When we finally reached the banks of the river where the tribe we wanted to visit lived, I was relieved. We set up tents, made a fire, ate and went to bed. I couldn't sleep and decided to take my torch, my Bible and a toilet roll. I walked up the riverbank passed the mouth of the ocean far away from the team. When I was far enough that nobody could hear me, I burst into tears. I needed to release all the emotions that I had experienced through the week and I needed God to help me. In that moment I cried out, "God please provide me with a husband, someone who would understand the delicate emotions of a woman, especially me – someone who would just take me in his arms and let me release my emotions." After an hour, a mostly used toilet roll and my Bible damped with tears, I returned to my tent. I was surrounded by tents of snoring men but I was too tired and too exhausted to care and I managed to sleep well that night. In the morning I felt a lot better and decided not to tell the rest of my team about my struggles from the day before.

The following night after eating the men made a huge fire on the beach. We decided to stand around it and spend time praying. Our day had been good, we had made some connections with the people using a translator and had set up a base from where we would run our different ministries. The last couple of days of rowing and getting settled had been full but we had not had much time with God. We felt we needed time to be refreshed by our Lord before beginning our different ministries of preaching, teaching and running children's programs. We sang worship songs that came to our minds and then waited quietly on God. Then it started to rain and one of the men in his prayer said, "I see Jesus, He is coming towards us. Cath he is coming towards you and just wants to hold you." I cannot explain it but I truly felt the presence of Jesus coming closer to me. In that moment my knees hit the beach sand and I wept. My team all came around me and held me. This made me cry even more. As they prayed for me I felt encouraged and understood. After our prayer time the men chatted to me and said that they finally saw that I was a normal woman and not some kind of superwoman. I explained how I didn't want to let them down as a team of men, but realized that it was also my own pride. As Jesus stripped my pride I could just be Cath, not "General Fitz" as I had become known among the team!

7 SIMPLY CATH

And He said to her, "Daughter, your faith has made you
well; go in peace, and be healed of your disease."
Mark 5:34

As the rain put out the glowing flames of our campfire,
and the last tendrils of smoke rose into the dark night sky,
the men all collapsed into their tents, fully clothed, but
exhausted after another day's hard work. I, too, was
exhausted, but unable to sleep, and so decided to take a
walk down the beach. I took off my shoes and allowed my
toes to squelch through the wet sand. After some time I
looked up and saw the most amazing sight. It was so
beautiful, the clouds had cleared away and the starry night
was spectacular. My heart was lighter and filled with love
and I praised God for comforting me and thanked him for
the team that had been so loving and understanding. I
started to pray for the people we came to minister to and
asked God to use us to touch their lives.

When I awoke the next morning I could hear the
crackling of the fire and the men quietly talking. I stepped
out of my tent and ate some breakfast of cooked oats and
dried fruit with the team. Feeling refreshed and ready I was
excited to see what God had in store for us that day. I
packed my bag fill of the supplies I had planned to use to
work with the children. Some of the team helped me and
we made our way to a nice shady patch under some trees.

We did not know the language so I pulled out some blow up balls for children to play with. In the beginning the children were terrified, most of them had not seen white people before, never mind big plastic things that grow when put on someone's mouth! One particular little girl was very brave and came towards us. I did not attempt to speak to her as I did not know her language, but tried to show her love through my eyes and actions. As we started to play with the ball together, slowly but surely the curiosity of the other children was greater than their fear. After a while we had quite a large crowd of children. Amongst my supplies were some huge A3 Bible story books with beautifully painted pictures. I had chosen different Bible stories that I felt might make an impact on the people of a rural, coastal fishing village. Our first story was the miracle of Jesus and the disciples when they went fishing. Manuel Bongo was my translator and he was brilliant, every action or dramatization I made when I told the story he did too with his translation. It was amazing to see the children's excitement about Jesus as they learnt how he filled the fishermen's nets. After a long day of games with the children, Bible stories and acting out the Bible stories I was exhausted. As I walked back to my tent I noticed the same little girl, who had first come to play with our blow up balls, was following me. I made signs that indicated that she should come to me, and together we walked hand in hand and I felt somehow that there was a bond between us. As the sun set, the sky was filled different shades of pinks and reds and it was beautiful. The evening sky became dark and the glow of the fire became like a magnet that attracted us all to sit around it. Some village people joined us and spontaneously began to sing and dance around the fire. The same little girl happened to be sitting next to me and she took my hand and beckoned me to come and dance with her. As I danced with her I was amazed at how God had created a bond between us. It was also incredible how God had opened the hearts of the people and they were dancing and celebrating with us. Actually it was a miracle that they did not reject us (who were strangers) or chase us as away, but welcomed us.

Each day more and more children joined our group and not only children but adults too. On our last day with them I had decided to use the Bible story of the woman who had had a discharge of blood for twelve years. The paintings in the large book were beautifully illustrated and in themselves explained the story of how Jesus healed this woman after she just touched his cloak. At the end of the story I invited people to come forward if they wanted prayer for healing and salvation. The first person to come up was this little girl who I had bonded with in the last couple of days. Her parents quickly followed and explained to Manuel my translator that her name was Cia and that she was completely deaf! As Manuel explained this to me my eyes welled up with tears and I held onto little Cia and we laid hands on her and prayed for Jesus to heal her. I had decided not to ask people after each prayer if they were healed but simply trusted that God in His power would do a work in each person we prayed for whether it was in that moment of our prayers or later. My heart was that God would receive all the glory and not us.

Some people also committed their lives to Jesus and a new little group of believers was forming. Early the next morning we had to leave, I left all my supplies with these wonderful people and hoped that they would be able to retell the stories to each other as they looked at the pictures. Our boats were packed and we paddled off while the group of people waved good-bye to us. I prayed that God would bring us back to these people one day as I watched their little figures become smaller and smaller along the beach where I had so often walked and poured out my heart to God.

God had heard my prayers and a couple of months later I found myself paddling along the same Zambezi

Delta again, this time enjoying the wild life more than before and very excited to meet Cia again. On our journey there we decided that we would stop for rests at other points where the fishermen stopped in their journeys along the river. Together with the translators the team explained the Bible story about how Jesus had taken some fishermen out to fish after they had fished all night and how Jesus had miraculously filled their nets full with fish. The men had never heard about Jesus before and when we were finished our story many came up asking questions. As our translator explained what they wanted we stood in shock and wondered how we were to answer their question. They were all asking us where this Jesus was, whether we had brought him with us and they all wanted to take him with them fishing the next morning! One of our team then explained how Jesus lived and died and rose again, how He set us free from the sin which we have and if we believe in Him we will be with him in heaven. Many people committed their lives to Jesus and I prayed that the next morning people would realize that Jesus was with each of them on their fishing boats and that he would provide them with all the fish they needed if they simply believed.

After four days of rowing, battling the tide and insects we made it back to our familiar beach where we had once been ministering to the people. This time many saw us coming from afar and came running to greet and welcome us. I was very eager to find Cia, and looked amongst each group of children to see if I could find her. When I started the children's program again I was sure she would be there but I could not find her. At the end of the day I was walking back to our tents with Manuel my translator and two women came towards me and fell on their knees before me. I could not understand what was going on. Then Manuel explained to me that they kept saying, "this is the woman that helped heal Cia and that God had opened her ears and she could hear!" I quickly pulled the women off their knees and told them that it was not me that healed Cia but Jesus. As I explained to them about Jesus and how he wanted to have a relationship with them they decided to remove their charms and traditional things from their arms and necks and committed their lives to Jesus. There were also men in this community that had also decided to commit their lives to Jesus so as a team we decided to have baptisms in the river and it was incredible to watch how Jesus had transformed so many lives. I never did see Cia again, her grandfather had taken her closer to town where he and his family could be part of a church and grow in her relationship with Jesus. I saw it as God's plan as I believe Cia knew it was Jesus that healed her and that God has just used me as His vessel. This time as we packed up our things to leave I realized that I might not have an opportunity to see these people again. I had a strong sense in my heart that God was calling me to unreached people, not just to spread His Word but also to disciple a people in their relationships with Jesus. I had a strong desire to live amongst a people, learn their language, their culture and bring Jesus into their lives. I prayed that God would lead me to a country and a people where He could use me, I prayed that on that journey God would provide me with friends, a team and if it was in his will a husband that I could work alongside in missions in unreached places.

8 TORIANA

Delight yourself in the Lord and he shall give you the
desires of your heart. Commit your way to the Lord, trust
also in Him, and He shall bring it to pass.

Psalm 37:4-5

The dry, open land spread before us and we were all happy
that we had come across the border with ease. I was sitting
in the very back of the Land-rover with some of the other
new team members, full of excitement for the venture we
had all embarked on in the Eastern Equatoria of South
Sudan. Our team was from all over the world, some from
America, some from Germany, a family from Kenya, an
Australian and myself, from South Africa. I had covered
myself with sun protection cream and now the dust from
our journey clung to my skin and face. But this didn't
bother me in the slightest as I thought about God's
amazing provision in the last year. I had had a dream a few
months before, about living amongst the unreached people
of Sudan. After praying about it with my mentor, family
and my missions sending cell from my church, within eight
months God had done the impossible and provided a way
to live amongst an unreached people-group in South
Sudan. African Inland Mission (AIM) had approached me
after I had shared a testimony of some of my mission work
and suggested I join their two year programme called

"Training in Ministry Outreach" (TIMO) After some paperwork and screening I was accepted. I needed to raise R30 000 to join this program but with God nothing is impossible and many were led by God to support me in this new venture. My church gave me their blessing and I was off again to a place and a people God was leading me to.

My thoughts about the amazing things God had done came to a sudden halt as I realized we were approaching a large river. Some of our team vehicles and trucks had gone before us and simply drove through the river. I was petrified and clung to the seat praying, but as we hit the river, the water seemed to part and although it rushed past just below the car windows, we made it through without incident! The more we travelled the more our journey involved rivers, slipping and sliding in mud and in parts non-existent roads. For the men on the team this was exciting and adventurous, for me it would take some time to get used to. I remembered how I had tried in previous mission trips to be "all tough" and this time reminded myself that I was simply Cath and that it was normal for me, a woman who had grown up in a city, to be overwhelmed by the journey and the rougher terrain I now inhabited. After about six hours we started driving into a mountainous region, green and lush. We waved at many groups of people along our way who were working in their fields. As we drove past them we could hear the echo of their greetings "Mong mong mong." The people seemed open and friendly and I was excited to live amongst them, learn their language and their culture.

The TIMO leadership team had in the last year prepared our mud houses in six different villages spread across some Lopit mountains. I, together with my American team mate, Jen, were to live in a village called Sohot. It was all about simple living, a long drop toilet, cold water bucket baths, no electricity, just an oil lamp each, no telephone or email. However, it was where we felt called and it was worth it. Our first three months were focused on learning the language and culture. This was a daunting task as the Lopit language had never been written; there was no alphabet or grammar book to lead us through what we needed to learn. We had to learn by hearing and observation. It was an incredible time as we began by learning the simple greetings and then learning how to ask someone their name and vice versa. One particular morning my neighbor Ihuhu called me and asked me to say my name. The more I said it and the more she tried to pronounce it the more she became convinced that I needed a new name, a Lopit name. At the time I was wearing a flowery hat and when she saw the hat she said: "Toriana!" In our villages things spread quickly by word of mouth and everyone came to know me as "Toriana" which I learnt means flower. The more I lived in Sudan the more I realized this name is true to who I am. I am a woman who loves Jesus and loves to serve, but as a woman I am also uniquely feminine and I like to do my hair and make myself look attractive. I had promised my grandmother that when I became a missionary I would do my best to look and act like a lady, taking care of my face, hair and nails. To some this may seem ridiculous but to me it became more and more important not to just be a simple missionary but to be a captivating one, like a beautiful flower for God's glory.

So with this in mind I continued with great faith living as Toriana amongst the Lopit people. Part of our training was to spend 10 days living with a family in another village. I lived with Basilio, his wife Dodu and children. My first task was to learn how to make a fire without paper or firelighters. After a couple of minutes the children could see I needed their help as I had been blowing so hard and was just making a lot of smoke which was burning my eyes and causing me to cry! So together we put some grass on the ashes of the previous night and they blew gently until the fire kindled and caught on the larger wood. Then the next task was walking to the river and fetching water. I was given a small 5 liter jerry can and the young girls all carried their 20 liter jerry cans. It was an exciting journey as we walked along little narrow paths under trees and through valleys. There were beautiful yellow and purple flowers along the way and I paused a minute or two to admire God's beauty. The closer we came I could hear the running water and the chatter of women to the left of me along the river and the laughter of men to the right down the river, below. They are very strict about bathing separately and for that I was most grateful! We filled our jerry cans at the spring up the river and then I joined the women in bathing at the river. For them it was strange to see a white naked woman and some smaller children had never seen a white woman so they hid behind rocks with their little eyes peering over to see if I behaved like the other women they knew. The other women felt more at ease to talk with me as I was doing the same activities that they were and felt freer to talk to me at the river than they had before. After bathing, my next task was to help weed their fields. After 2 hours my hands were bleeding but I was determined to continue to be a part of learning the culture. Chopping wood was important in preparing for the fire for the meal for the day, so I attempted to level an ax above my head and chop the wood like I had seen the women do so easily. After about an hour my fingers had blisters and I had only chopped a small amount of wood. My respect for the women grew each day as I realized how much they had to do. In the final days of this hectic training I was brought a chicken that I was told I needed to learn how to slaughter. Dodu explained what I had to do as she prepared a pot of boiling water and my task was, seemingly, simple. Hold the chicken down, slit its neck and put it in the boiling hot water. Easier said than done! So I mustered all my energy and emotions and with a shaking hand managed to slit the chicken's neck, and cut its head right off. There was a lot of blood so I quickly ran and placed the chicken in the hot pot. Within seconds, the chicken, minus its head, jumped straight out of the hot pot and ran wildly in circles! I took no time to hang around, screamed and ran off the compound! The shrieks of laughter that came from the women and children who were watching could be heard all the way down the valley. Dodu called me back and told me she would continue the job of getting the chicken ready. I was greatly relieved and sat with the children and played with them. The experience had given new meaning to the English expression, "Running around like a chicken without a head"! After an hour or two we could smell the delicious chicken and the children were excited for the meal ahead. In normal circumstances I would have been excited too, but had to muster up strength to eat this poor chicken that I had killed. At first it was hard, but in a few minutes I was able to enjoy the meal too.

When I finally climbed under my mosquito net and into my sleeping bag, on my last night with this family, I realized how different our lives are. We can simply go to the Supermarket and buy a chicken, switch on the oven, spice the pre-cleaned chicken without a head and put it in the oven. We can then take a nice clean hot shower and within a couple of hours eat a roasted chicken without much work at all.

I lay thinking of all the relationships that had grown deeper in the two weeks because I had worked alongside the people and was learning about them and their culture. I realized how it had helped me learn a lot of their language and it had also opened their hearts to me. I prayed that their hearts would remain open to me for when the time came that I had enough of their language to be able to share what Jesus had done on the cross for them. With that thought and prayer I drifted into a deep sleep.

The next morning I was sad to say goodbye to this family but very excited to be back in my mud house in my village, Sohot. The two plate gas stove, the long drop toilet and the bucket bath using the rainwater from our large rainwater tank – all seemed an incredible luxury. I thanked God for all of it and enjoyed soaking my feet, painting my nails and combing my wet hair smelling of my shampoo. Yes, I was living in the Sudan mountains' with the Lopit people, living a simple life, but it was also good to spend some time being me and enjoy some of the things that made me feel like Toriana!

9 THE DRAMA QUEEN

Weeping may endure for a night, but joy cometh in the morning.
Psalm 30:5

The sky was dark and the night had been quiet. It all began with one deathly scream from a hut below our village. I shot up from my bed and called over our mud wall to my housemate Jen, "what's going on down there?" We both put our material wraps around our waists and sandals on our feet, with torches in our hands we quickly went outside. More screams could be heard from the compound of Alberto. We rushed down, as did many others. As we arrived some were sitting swaying backwards and forwards groaning and others came throwing themselves on the floor wailing. Alberto's wife, who was known as being the drama queen of the village, had started the wailing that had sent the message to all around that he had died. We sat quietly as we tried to understand what was going on. Then we heard people whispering that Alberto had just died! The more we sat there the more Jen was convinced that he was not dead. We were torn between respecting the culture and the mourning process and the fact that he could be alive and Jen, who was a nurse, could help him.

Some of the men in the group may have overheard

Jen and I talking, as slowly they began to realize that Alberto might, in fact, not be dead after all. Jen managed at that point to take a look at him, and realized that Alberto most likely had a slipped disk in his back, or something similar, which had caused him to pass out from the pain. Suddenly he appeared to be coming around again! Before Jen had a chance to tell the men to be careful how they moved Alberto, they lifted him by his arms and legs, causing him to scream out in pain. In an instant, the wailing and crying from the group stopped, and people sat in stunned silence, some thinking he'd come back from the dead and others not knowing what to think at all. Personally, I was quite relieved that the villagers had not yet decided to dig a hole and bury him. I had heard so many horror stories of missionaries standing by in an effort to respect the culture, and watching while someone was buried alive. Thankfully this was not to be the case that evening and Jen and I could return to our hut knowing that the crisis was over.

Living in a Lopit village meant that we often experienced events or happenings that were very foreign to our own culture. Often, the young girls of the village would make up a song that replayed an incident that happened and would sing it and dance it in the village dance area under the full moon. These were a people that had no written language and therefore no books. It was only their traditions, song and dance that kept their culture alive. It was through these experiences that I found a key to reaching the hearts of these lovely people and it evolved into an idea of creating a drama with song and dance with different messages from the Bible. However, I could not do this alone so I shared my idea with the team and asked them if any of them were interested in acting or helping me with putting on a drama.

There was a particular man on our team that was very quiet. Whenever he shared something with us it was well thought out and significant. He was very happy serving each member on the team, and whether it was carrying a gas bottle or washing dishes, he was quietly working behind the scenes. On the day that I shared my idea about putting together a drama of Bible stories, he was the first to volunteer. I was amazed and could not quite imagine how such a shy and quiet person would manage on a drama team, but I decided to give him a chance. I prepared the scripts for each actor and we started putting together the drama for the youth of the church. In the practices this "mystery man" seemed pretty good and the other actors were also doing well. However, on the day of the performance he swept me off my feet! When he was before an audience he became the actor he was chosen to be and was absolutely brilliant and funny all at once. I and the other actors were shocked, as we knew him so differently, but the audience were absolutely enthralled by him and just loved it when he came on stage. His name was Martin, he was German, but could speak English and he became our new drama King!

The more I choreographed dramas, the more he became one of the main actors in each performance. I became pleasantly surprised when I arrived at each practice that Martin had prepared chairs and got everybody ready for the practice. He encouraged me a lot in this ministry. Then he started helping me in all my ministry areas, when I arrived for Sunday school I found he had swept the classroom and brought some benches inside for the children. I started confiding in Martin more and more and he soon became a good friend.

At some point in the months following the creation of our drama group, a teammate of mine, Pattie, and I decided to help Martin with his "farm". This was his ministry to the people and he attempted to grow vegetables and fruit for the team. Pattie and I used every Tuesday and Thursday after teaching at school to help him in his field.

One particular week most of our team were going on a shopping run to Uganda. Jen and I had asked Martin to please look after our cat Jazzie and to check on the house, which he happily agreed to do. While we were away I felt led to buy him a few gifts to thank him for his help and friendship. I knew he was a very spiritual man and liked creative things, so I decided to buy him a variety of little gifts, all of which had some connection to the armor of God mentioned in Ephesians 6. His parcel consisted of a sunhat for the helmet of salvation, a nice new leather belt, a tie for the breastplate of righteousness and socks for the readiness to go forward with God's word in a comfortable way! When we arrived back and I gave him the gift he was a bit shocked but seemed happy. The next day he asked me if I normally bought gifts for people and I replied that if I was inspired to I would. It seemed that this gift sparked something in Martin that caused him to pray a lot. We remained good friends, but I had to really discipline myself as my feelings for him were growing stronger and I kept praying that the Lord would remove this temptation from me and that he would help me to remain focused on Him and the ministry that I was doing in Sudan.

Two years prior to this moment I had started a dairy, which I dedicated to my future husband. Each time I was inspired to pray or write a scripture for my future husband - I wrote it in this book for him. I knew and trusted that God had someone in mind for me. The more I was with Martin, the more I knew that he was the one for me, but my personality is a passionate, loving and outgoing one and I felt I was becoming too overwhelming for Martin. The following is an entry from my dairy to my future husband, dated 7th May 2007:

> "I have discovered that I love working alongside you in the garden and with God praying that things will grow. I loved doing 'plays' with you – you are truly a gifted man. I couldn't resist buying you gifts in Uganda…but perhaps you found me too forward I am not sure…but I feel very proud when I see you wearing my hat. Martin I do believe God is opening my eyes…a life partner is more than passion, romance and love…it's about being partners accomplishing things for God. I see you as my Boaz if that's O.K. and will wait patiently for God to move in you and I. Martin I am afraid to 'love' at the moment its scary for me because I have been rejected so many times. The Lord is the one who has sustained me and kept me a virgin but he knows my heart and the key that fits. I hope that key is you, as I long to be your Ruth!"

I did not realize that the team was watching how our behavior changed towards each other. People saw how we looked at each other at team events and meetings, and somehow when love is growing between two people there is no way of hiding it. The two men living with Martin said they found it strange that for months Martin was never interested in talking on the radio when one of us from the other houses came on line. But now whenever I came on the radio Martin would dash out of his room and grab the radio to ensure that he was the one who answered. Then suddenly one day I found the following letter from Martin hidden in one of my books. This is how it read:

24/6/2007

"Dear Toriana, I'm glad and grateful to God that you are back safely and as Craig told me had a good, blessed and joyful time with the women!

Thanks to you also for borrowing me this valuable book. Have you already found your future role in the Lopit community after being a learner? The book has good advices, challenges – may be I can read it any time later....

...For today I would like to share a parable from the depth of my heart with you. This word from Isaiah could be the key to your understanding...

...Okay, today one month ago, I discovered during my birthday quiet time in the mountain river, that a planting in my heart had started germinating. I don't know for how long, but I believe with a lot of prayer you have sown a seed of God's love, affection, interest, and care. When I discovered this germinating seed I rejoiced and tended to see in it another miracle of God's love arising in me. And believe it or not I care and pray about this strange plant daily. I don't know what kind of plant it is and what will it look like in a later stage. Sometimes I'm not sure – is it a weed or a wonderful flower for God's glory and peoples joy and blessing? Would you Toriana like to help me identify this not yet unfolded plant? So far for now I would like to share with you 3 words from our Father which were comforting and directing me during the last days: Isaiah 43:19a:

"Behold I do a new thing...now it shall spring forth. Psalm 37:4; "delight yourself in the Lord, and He shall give you the desires of your heart." Hosea 6:1-3; "Come let us return to the Lord, for He has torn, but he will heal us, He has stricken, but he will bind us up. After 2 days he will revive us. On the 3rd day He will raise us up, that we may live in His sight. Let us know, let us pursue the knowledge of the Lord. Yours Martin"

I read the letter and scriptures over and over again and they brought such joy to my heart. I could understand how the letter and scriptures from Isaiah and Psalms fitted into our future lives together but I could not understand how the Hosea scripture fitted into our future and so I left this one up to God to show me!

I was so excited and thought of a creative way to give Martin his answer to the letter he had written me. It was a Sunday and I knew that he would not be on his farm on Sunday – so I wrote a letter with a picture of a flower and found a tree at the entrance to his farm that I knew he would pass. I taped the message to the tree and prayed that no one would take it. This was my reply to him:

"Dearest Martin

My response to your parable is that we are going to be a flower for God's glory and like seedlings need time to grow so I believe we need the time to grow as you and God lead us. Yours Toriana."

That night I could not sleep and prayed that the Lord would protect the message I had put on the tree. I knew I would only see him in two days' time and I hoped and prayed he would find the message.

10 MEIN SCHATZ

The voice of my beloved! Behold he comes
Leaping upon the mountains,
Skipping upon the hills.

Song of Solomon 2:8

Early in the morning, a day after leaving the note for Martin attached to the tree at the entrance of his farm, I lay tossing and turning and unable to sleep anymore. Eventually I decided to take my Bible and go to the place where I often had my 'quiet time.' I set off in the dark to the little hill behind the Sohot village, knowing that I would soon have a good view of the sunrise, one of my favorite times of day. Often I took my little iPod with a range of worship music on it, and this morning was no exception. I felt inspired to really praise God with all that was in me, and so I removed the wrap that I wore as a makeshift skirt from around my waist and stood dancing in my tracksuit pants and shirt as the sun began rising. Little did I know that Martin was having his quiet time on the opposite mountain and saw me as a tiny figure across the valley dancing on top of the mountain. When I had finished my time of praise and worship I sat down on a rock to admire the beauty of God's creation around me. Suddenly, something caught my eye, as I noticed someone across the valley from me on the opposite hill waving a white bag and signaling a greeting to me. I soon realized it was Martin and jumped up, grabbing my colorful wrap, to begin signaling back. I felt such joy, and then overwhelming embarrassment, as I realized that Martin might have been watching my wild praise, worship and dancing routine! Once we had finished signaling our greeting, I watched Martin as he walked down the mountain to his house. I knew he would be in charge of preparing the daily breakfast porridge for his housemates, and as I sat there, I continued to pray, asking God what he had in store for Martin and I. I did not see Martin at all that day, but waited eagerly to hear his voice on the radio that evening, as we were in the habit of sharing news between households and villages on a daily basis. When he called it was wonderful to hear his voice but I realized the rest of the team was listening to our call so I could not ask him if he had received my note that I had left for him on the tree on his farm. I tried to surreptitiously ask how his day had been and he replied that it was a very good day, but I was not sure if that was because he had read my note or had just had a good day farming. My curiosity had to wait yet another day!

The next morning after school I decided to go to Martin's farm a few minutes before Pattie. As I arrived on Martin's farm he said to me: "Cath I really liked the surprise you left for me on the tree." I said nothing, but just looked him in the eyes, and it seemed that both of us knew at that moment that something special was happening. I was so excited! We both then agreed that Martin needed to talk to our team leader and the leaders of the training program and that I couldn't meet him on the farm alone anymore unless there was a group of people with me. In this cultural context it would not be appropriate for a man and a woman to be alone in a field unless they were married. We had already completed the first year of our training program and knew that for another year we would only be able to share our love through letters until the two-year program was completed. I wondered how I was going to be able to wait a whole year before I could hold Martin's hand or even kiss him; I prayed with all my heart that God would help me. It was December 2007, our relationship had begun, and continued over the next few months through a variety of notes and letters. So our love began and continued through love letters:

31st December 2007

My dearest beloved Cath, praise God for his leading. On Saturday in my quiet time in the "green cathedral" (Martin's quiet time place amongst the trees, near his home) I was challenged to start praying for our children, God knows them already and our hearts should be prepared and full of love and patience when they enter our lives. I praise God for an extra-ordinary year...you surprised me with a heart-warming song through the radio! I miss you. Yours Martin

This letter really touched my heart as I had longed and prayed not only for a husband but for children too, a family of my own. I had been sharing over email with my dad about our growing relationship and my dad felt it was time for him to meet Martin. It was in March 2008 when my dad flew to Kenya during our two week's break to be with us both. My dad's first concern was that Martin was more than ten years older than me. I tried to explain in words to my dad that I really felt this man was the one for me but realized that my dad would have to spend time with him before he was convinced that Martin was worthy of his precious daughter! To my surprise my dad and Martin got on really well, I had thought my dad would have kept his prejudice about our age difference but he didn't. My dad also watched me when I was with him and saw that he really made me happy. Then my dad asked me one evening while I was preparing dinner for us all, " Cath, you really love him don't you?" My response was an unequivocal "Yes, Dad I truly love him deeply." During this two-week period we all knew that Martin needed to ask my dad if he could have my dad's blessing to marry me but it was very stressful for him to find the right moment to ask him.

Martin's words written below in our mutual diary. (We decided to start this diary so we could write our feelings and thoughts on different days. In this way we could share our deepest thoughts even when we could not be together alone.):

15th-21st March 2008

We had now moved to Tinderet and praise God the journey was a wonderful special time with you as a reliable co-driver. We enjoyed with your dad lunch near the equator, a lovely picnic place in the forest. The guesthouse in Tinderet was a wonderful place where we had nightly log fires and evenings of laughter as the three of us read the book called "Covenant Marriage" by Gary Chapman. Praise God for the time I have not laughed so much in a long time…now it is everywhere known we have a common future in our hearts. You came with me for planting maize at the dam – and really my beloved you do a good job, in assisting me well in driving. It's so wonderful to work together with you in the fields.

22nd March
Today was a special day for us (and your dad) I promised to help in planting maize again on the Monkey farm. I fought to come home early enough for a swim together with you in the pool – and it was a really a great joy. You prepared delicious milkshakes and with God's help I finally asked your dad, whether he was willing to release his dearest daughter into my care and responsibility. Praise God he knew me, my struggle already and had released you already in his heart so he gave his blessing joyfully and in prayer. Thank you my dearest for your accompanied prayers!!! Moments I will not forget for months or even longer: your dad passing through the airport check giving me his last greetings and command from now on to take care of you, my

dearest from God and your dad entrusted one!!! I saw the great responsibility, was fully aware of the gift and agreed! I love and miss your dad and enjoyed how he left into the body of the airplane waiving his hand towards us."

I can remember that moment too and it was a moment in time where I realized that my dad was officially letting me go. I realized in that moment that there would be no more phone calls or emails sharing my heart deeply with my dad and asking his advice. My dad in that moment had passed that responsibility to Martin. I should have been so happy and excited but I can remember crying all the way home in the car. My dad had let go of me, now it was time for me to let go of him. Martin really cared for me in this time and wrote me this little poem:

You are my God given treasure
A wonderful gift hard to measure
I love you when you weep
from your heart so deep
I love you when you laugh
Even when sometimes life is tough

Through the experience with my dad Martin saw how important it was to honor our parents. So we also desired to honor Martin's parents, Helmut and Lilli. Therefore we decided that we would not become officially engaged until after I had come to Germany, spent time with Martin's family and church. So we planned to go to Germany for Christmas 2008. While we waited and served our Lord in Sudan our love and anticipation grew for what was to come. Martin and I continued to write letters filled with love and passion as we waited patiently until Christmastime.

24th May 2008

My precious Schatz, dearest Cath,

"Lord you have assigned me my portion and my cup, you have made my lot secure. You have granted me a beautiful portion surely I have delighted in your inheritance. Therefore my heart is glad and my tongue rejoices, my body will also rest secure because you will not abandon me to the grave nor will you let your Holy One see decay. You have made known to me the path of Life. You will fill me with joy in your presence with eternal pleasure at your right hand. (Psalm 19:5-6, 9-11)

Those words in Psalms touched my heart in those days with praise and gratitude to God. He has encouraged me with His Words and I really see how gracious He is to me how manifold He has blessed me!!! And you are my beloved Cath, a very special portion which God has granted to me. I'm full of joy today, because I am reminded again and again about the second largest miracle in my life(the first is of course his life in Jesus): your presence, committed love and help, faithfulness, encouragement and friendship towards me. My heart is full of praises towards God, because of this miracle. I couldn't recognize it yet one year ago as He revealed it's truth as I trusted the Lord and we made mutual steps towards each other in prayer and learning to know each other. Through your precious notes I was reminded about the initial picture of a seed in our hearts, unknown whether it would develop into a weed or a flower, a precious beautiful flower for His glory. I would describe our status that we are not yet united and not yet flourishing but I see blossoms developing and although I haven't seen us as a flower but I believe one day it will open up and show it's beauty and give praise to God. I think still that we move by faith and look forward with hope and joy. But my faith has grown, that God has already a very good purpose, His purpose as He leads us together! As I praise God standing on a big rock, I saw on a tree next to me those blossoms which you see in the grinding stone sink and took it as a symbol, a gift of confirmation from God to share with you the joy God's common gift in our hearts!

My dearest Cath, thank you so much that you served me today, that my birthday became a day of joy and thankfulness! You overwhelmed me with your creativity, useful gifts and wonderful picture and notes, your snack here and wonderful precious love in many ways and situations of my life. God bless you richly! I really love you deeply! In love and thanks yours Martin.

11 RUTH

13 June 2007

My dearest beloved Schatz

A wife of noble character is her husbands' crown, but a disgraceful wife is like decay in his bones

Proverbs 12:4

I am not a king but with you my dearest Cath I will wear a permanent crown in my life! I praise God for you! You really enrich my life wonderfully. Besides God there is nobody to whom I can open to in the same way as you. "

18 August 2007

"My dearest Cath,
…I dare to tell you Cath I love you so much in everything even in the things I do not know yet! Thank you for your confidence and trust in me. I appreciate it highly with love and respect! May God bless my dearest Cath richly today, yours deep in love Martin."

I had a huge beautifully-white thick cotton-woven cloak that Martin used in our dramas when he was acting the role of Jesus. He loved this cloak and asked if he could have it to sleep in. I happily agreed to let him have it and told him that one day when we are married it would be big enough for us to share. The next day he wrote this note in our mutual diary...

23 September 2007

"In the warm night I used the wonderfully gentle and huge cloak for covering my body but in the morning my dearest Ruth was not found..." (In this diary entry Martin is making reference to a story about Ruth from the Bible. It begins as a tragic story with Ruth becoming a widow and ends with her meeting Boaz and their marriage)

Every letter that Martin wrote romanced me and drew me closer to him each month. I desperately wanted to run into his arms, have him hold me, have his hands touch my hair and face and then... I prayed many a time for God to help me wait until it was His timing that we came together as one. For a year and a half we had kept a mutual dairy which we exchanged each week and wrote our deepest thoughts, passions and desires. At the back of the diary we had a page with 3 columns one for kisses, one for hugs and one for back massages. Each time one of us felt the desire to hug or give one another a kiss or back massage we would write it in our dairy. In our waiting we wanted to honor the culture in Lopit, Sudan and Kenya and did not want to become physically involved until after we were married.

Above our human passions and desires was our love

and relationship with Jesus and our hearts were also passionate about loving and reaching out to the Lopit people in South Sudan. During 2007 -2008 Martin felt led to visit another village about half a day's walk from our area. He went alone and found pathways to reach it. There was a man named pastor Peda who was trying to start a new church in this village called Ohilang. Martin felt led to support and encourage him to start a church. He faithfully went to Ohilang by foot every second weekend and this new work was very much part of our prayers. In May he tried to ride to Ohilang by bicycle.

Our Mutual Diary

18 May 2008

"My dearest Cath,
I had a wonderful day with Mark riding with bicycles, my first time in Sudan. We went to his home village Ohilang passed Ebacure and Iboni. I was grateful that you had peace staying behind with Sunday school and drama kids. God gave us good opportunities to reach many people. I got a taste and desire in our future common ministry to reach in that way people in remote villages, like Ohilang. Was happy to hear your voice on the radio in the evening. Yours in love Martin"

I was very excited about the growing work that Martin was pursuing in Ohilang and prayed with him that when we returned after our visit in Germany and marriage in South we could visit and begin a work together in Ohilang. I had a longing desire to meet these people but knew I could not go alone with Martin by foot or on bicycle as it would be seen as a scandal within the community for an unmarried man and woman walking off into the bush alone! But I prayed that God would one day give me an opportunity to see the new work Martin had spent a year or two working on. He had spent a lot of time and energy building relationships and helping establish the church there. Two other missionary men from Martin's mission – DIGUNA (Die Guten Nachrit für Afrika – The good news for Africa) were serving with us in the Lopit Mountains in the last months of 2008. They were Jürgen and Tobi. It was really a joy for Martin to have them staying with him in our last months in Sudan before flying to Germany. We decided together that we would like to visit Ohilang with Martin. I was thrilled and it was such a joy to finally meet Pastor Peda, his wife and family and the small, growing church. We also did a tour around the village and met other people there too. All the children were very friendly towards Martin but some of them had never seen a white woman before and after seeing me one or two screamed and ran away. It took a while for the children to come close to me and when they did they would run towards me touch my arm and then quickly run away. I thought that I must look like a white ghost to them.

After our time together in Ohilang we then spent some time preparing for our long journey from Sudan to Germany. I was so excited that the time would soon come where we could hold hands freely, embrace one another and kiss.

About once every four months Martin would write a newsletter to his family and friends in Germany. He was a very good farmer but struggled with typing on a computer. I became his faithful secretary who typed his newsletters and emailed them for him. He told me many a time how grateful he was that I could help him in this way. The newsletters Martin hand written in the past were with very small print. He wrote as small as he could so he could put as much as he could on one page. I heard from many people that they had to enlarge his newsletters on a photocopy machine so they could read them. He had served with DIGUNA in Kenya for three years before coming to Sudan and in Kenya it was still possible for him to post his newsletters. But now in Sudan there was not a possibility at all to post them and he had to rely on me to email them for him. Some people missed Martins personal touch in his hand written newsletters but others were happy that they could finally read his letters without having to enlarge the writing. In one of his newsletters Martin had tried to prepare his family and friends in Germany before our coming about our relationship, which he asked me to type and email.

17 May 2008

My dearest beloved Cath

I was so grateful that you made so many efforts for designing and typing my German info letter in which I announced our friendship to my friends, church and prayer partners in the pattern of a riddle. You sacrificed a lot of time and creative power...I love you so much and appreciate your extra mile, thus you've got a kiss on our list!

Thankfully I did not have to wait much longer to claim that kiss as we planned to personally meet my family, friends and prayer supporters during the month of August 2008 in South Africa. You would think that after over a year of waiting the moment we stepped off the plane in South Africa we would have embraced and kissed right there at the airport. We had become so used to being together without holding hands, embracing or kissing that it felt perfectly normal not to, but we were also feeling overwhelmed by the western South African culture. I can remember us both coming out of the cloakrooms shocked that there were no taps for us to wash our hands. Martin said he had spent a long time looking for the tap to wash his hands and decided to wait until we got home. Thankfully there was another lady in the ladies' cloakroom and I saw her wave her hands under the outlet pipe and then the water came out as a laser had read her hand movements. I explained this to Martin and we realized that we had become used to the simple life in Sudan and that it would take us time to adjust to all the new things in the western world.

We had been in South Africa a week and I had really enjoyed walking with Martin in parks hand in hand. I was thankful to God that we had waited because each time I felt his big gentle hand hold my small delicate hand, it was special and unique and I prayed a small prayer of thanks for the love we had. I will never forget the 9th August as we had walked a long walk through the Bordeaux Park and decided to talk about what kissing meant to each of us. We had become so used to writing letters and talking about everything before we did anything that it seemed natural to talk about this too. Then Martin turned and pulled me towards himself, his hands gently taking the hair off my face, looking deeply into my eyes, his arms now enveloping me, our hearts both racing and as I closed my eyes I felt his lips touching mine.

We spent two months (August- September 2008) in South Africa giving reports about our work in Sudan and Martin spent time getting to know my family and friends. We then returned to Sudan to continue our mission work until Christmas-time. Just before Christmas, 20th December 2008 we planned to leave Sudan and fly to Germany so I could meet Martin's family and friends.

My time for day-dreaming about the past was over and I had to get back to packing. Looking forward I had butterflies in my stomach the whole time as I contemplated what it would be like to meet Martin's friends and family, and I couldn't speak a word of German so I was nervous about this aspect of our journey too. I can clearly remember Martin bringing me a freshly picked bouquet of flowers when we arrived in Kenya, after our three day's journey by road from Sudan. He always liked to pray that God would help him find the most beautiful flowers he could present to me. I received them with much joy and then Martin told me I would not be getting flowers for a long while. He explained that through winter in Germany it was too cold for flowers and he refused to spend any money on flowers from a flower shop!

When we eventually arrived in Germany, Martin's church friends, Thomas and Susanne, met us at the airport. I was pleasantly surprised to see that Susanne spoke good English and they really made me feel welcome. I also so enjoyed meeting the rest of Martin's church family and friends and wherever we went I felt totally loved and accepted. After meeting some of Martin's friends we made the long train trip to Nürnburg to meet his parents.

It was an incredible time and even though we could not communicate well there was a growing love between us. It was also exciting to meet his sister Claudia and her daughter Helena. They all made me feel special and part of the family. I particularly enjoyed seeing was the slideshows of Martin from when he was a baby, their family holidays in the mountains and learning more about how Martin grew up.

After about two weeks spent with Martin's family, on the 6th January 2009, Martin took me on a surprise cross-country skiing adventure. This was my first time to ski so Martin and his parents decided that I should use what they call ski-walking skis with special skis where you can lift your heal. Below is what I wrote to family and friends at the time.

Martin led me on skis for the first time through beautiful white snow. It was a cold 6th January 09 day, -7 degrees C! We went through wonderful white fern-tree cathedrals and then climbed to 'Signalstein'(Signal Rock). Long ago 'Signalstein' was the watching point for the surrounding castles. If any enemies were spotted the man on watch would light a large fire on this 'Signalstein' to alert the watchmen at the castles. It was on this 'Signalstein' that Martin with emotion in his eyes asked me to be his wife…my response was that I would love to be his wife. We embraced with a kiss that warmed both our icy lips! Later Martin presented me with a beautiful engagement ring. We plan to have a small wedding on the

5th April 2009 with close family and friends at Carmel in George.

So we had great plans and spent the next days and weeks preparing wedding invitations and finalizing our wedding plans. I was due to fly back to South Africa on the 20 February to prepare myself, my wedding dress and other details and then Martin would join me a month later. During our time of travels seeing friends and family in Germany Martin was not feeling well. At first we thought it could be malaria or a tropical disease that he had picked up in Sudan and we had been to many different doctors, who all conducted various tests in an attempt to diagnose what exactly was wrong with Martin. In this time I also noticed and found it strange that Martin did not want to be as affectionate with me as we had been in South Africa. I thought perhaps it was the German culture to not be so affectionate in public, or perhaps Martin did not want us to fall into temptation or sin before we were married. I liked to be shown love through physical touch, whereas Martin enjoyed quality time. So for him it was not so difficult to not receive love through touch, at least that is what I thought. What I did not realize was that Martin was struggling with something that he did not know how to share with me. He had told me about a strange bulge forming above his private parts and we had thought that it might be a hernia. What was also happening is that there seemed to be more estrogen forming in his body, which meant that the normal functions of his body as man were no longer there. This is what he was afraid to tell me. During his medical check-ups they realized that he needed a hernia operation and suggested to us that he have the operation before marriage and not after. So we planned for him to have the operation on the 10th February. I was with him in the hospital and the doctors told him that it would be a quick routine procedure, lasting approximately 30 minutes. After he was taken into the operating theatre, I waited and waited and waited and inside of me I knew there was something wrong but I did not know what it was. After a wait of over three hours, Martin was finally wheeled out of theatre, attached to a number of different drips and machines, some of which were apparently for pain management. He looked like he was in so much pain and I could not help him. I stayed with him, held his hand and prayed. He could only speak German to me at the time and I tried my best to understand him. I made different cards for him with German Scriptures and posted them around his bed. I tried to ask the nurses and doctors what was going on but I could not speak German and they could not speak good enough English to explain. They keep taking him for me tests and then a CT scan and this all took time. A few days later we received the news that they had found cancer in Martin's body. They found cancer in his brain, in his lungs and stomach – they told us there was no hope and they were not sure how much longer he had to live. We held each other's hands tightly in disbelief. In front of the doctor I told Martin that I loved him and still wanted to marry him until death parted us.

After the doctor left the room Martin looked at me and said; "Cath, I don't want to marry you anymore." I held his hands with tears in my eyes and asked him why. He said he did not want to make me a widow, I told him we had started a love story together and that I wanted to finish it with him. Then with embarrassment and pain he looked at me and said; "Cath, I cannot offer you sex!" In that moment I came to him and held him and said; "mein Schatz, I want to marry you because I love you and not because of sex." Then a pastor named David came in and had felt led by the Holy Spirit to come and visit Martin even though he did not know him. He took both our hands and focused on Martin, speaking Scriptures of hope and love and I saw joy returning to Martin'.

Once he left Martin called his mother to tell her the news. Martin found telling his mother the news terribly hard and wept afterwards on his pillow. As I held him and asked him what he was feeling he said that he didn't want to cause pain to the people he loved. In the midst of this hard time we also knew that I would have to leave Germany because my visa was expiring. Martin's dad phoned me and begged me to stay but I had no choice but to return to South Africa and trust God to provide. I knew when I arrived in South Africa I would have to phone the church and all the places we had booked to cancel our wedding plans in South Africa as Martin was not allowed to fly as flying in his current condition was out of the question. The night before I left Germany it was late and I was tired. Martin took my hand and drew me to himself, gently stroked my face and hair, enveloped his arms around me and passionately kissed me. With tears in my eyes I asked him why he had not kissed me like that before in Germany and he said that he didn't think I would want to marry a sick man but now he saw the truth that I truly loved him for who he was no matter how sick he became. He also said that he was not sure if we would see each other again and without any more words we continued to embrace and kiss each other and I wished that the time would never pass.

Leaving Martin and Germany was the hardest thing I have ever done and I placed all my tears and prayers in God's hands as I trusted Him that He would help me to return and see Martin again. When the officials at the German Embassy in South Africa heard my story they too became emotional and somehow God moved their hearts together with the embassy in Germany and they made an exception VISA for me. In addition to that I discovered that in Germany people who wanted to get married had to get legally married in a court first before marrying in church. This meant that if I wanted to marry Martin I would have to supply seven different documents from different South African government departments. Normally this could take up to three months! Katha, a friend from DIGUNA based in Germany at the time, worked very hard with the embassy and court to help me from the German side with all the papers. I will always be grateful for her help at that time. God is a God of wonders and in just ten days I had my VISA to return and all the documents required for marriage in Germany.

I couldn't wait to return and was also aware that many people all over the world were praying for us both. I was also grateful for my many new found friends in DIGUNA Germany like Corinna and Ute, Jo and Anna Hummel and our friends from the Altenkirchen Church Thomas and Susanne and many others who walked this road with us.

The dressmaker had finished my wedding dress to take with me, and I had my plane ticket and was so excited to return to Germany. When I arrived at the airport it was just wonderful to be met by Martin with a bunch of flowers (bought from a flower shop!) and Corinna from DIGUNA. We embraced with joy! Martin then took my hand and I felt things were different. He was so proud to walk in public hand in hand with me. When I arrived I found a beautiful card, which must have taken hours for him to write, and then he told me to dress up for the evening as he was taking me out to a Chinese restaurant for dinner.

After the dinner Martin asked me how I was feeling and I told him that I was more in love with him than ever before. We then embraced for a long time and thanked God that he had allowed us to be together again, that He had moved mountains for us so that we could continue our love- story together until God decided to heal him or take him home.

12 FRAU BEZOLD

To my dearest beloved Catherine Fitzpatrick
11 Jean Avenue
Bordeaux
Johannesburg
South Africa

Haiger,
25 February 2009

My dearest beloved friend Cath,
I've joy, hope and peace in the Lord and whenever my thoughts
wander to you I rejoice always in prayer and thanksgiving for you –
the gracious gift of Him! He answers prayers when we come before
Him and as you prayed on the phone He is already working in me,
my body before we realize it! Beside other scriptures Isaiah 41,10-13
encouraged me today – given by Helmut and Ulrike (Music leaders
of the choir in Wimmer!) There is no fear because God only wants to
help us, read also today - "Prayer" is not to break God's resistance
but to utilize His willingness…. dearest Cath be blessed like me as
you are a part of me and deserve to share everything of my life. I love
you and miss you in pre-joy yours Martin.

This was a postcard that Martin sent me while I was in
South Africa for the ten days waiting for my visa and
documents for marriage. I can remember my dad coming
into my room with the postcard and saying that he had
never seen a postcard addressed in that way and he was

amazed that the postman could read and understand where it should be delivered with such a title. We both laughed because we knew Martin well, especially his sense of humour. I was so encouraged and surprised to receive this postcard from Germany. It is true that when we pray and have faith, we are trusting in God for those things that we do not yet see or have. Martin and I both longed to be married and with faith, love and hope we prayed.

When I arrived in Germany and was embraced by Martin his physical appearance had changed. As a result of the cancer, he was required to take strong steroid drugs in an attempt to reduce the fluid build up and subsequent pressure in his brain. This meant that his head was quite swollen, as were his eyes, but I immediately noticed the same look of love that I had got used to, this time even more intense than before. We embraced each day as a gift from God to both of us and we were determined to enjoy every moment we had. Below is the card I found in my postbox in Germany when I arrived.

9 March 2009

My dearest beloved Cath,

Praise God our heavenly Father that He has kept us safe and secure in His mighty arms during our separation!!! I'm so glad that you are back now and that he opened a quick way for your return! I missed you for sure although His omnipresence was so obvious and so much comforting! Jesus is my closest friend and I'm grateful that He has given me in His grace you as my beloved companion by my side. This is still a miracle an underserved gift from His loving hands and I never want to stop praising and thanking Him for you! For sure, I sense the coming time will be not easy for us. The effects of the radiation and the medication and later chemo will handicap me more and more and it will be hard to participate in your personal needs. I love you so much Cath and I will be here for you to hold you and encourage you in your faith and in all activities you will do for my benefit. I'm sure of your love, of your commitment and faithfulness! I'm proud of you. Your life is really a shining testimony! The people here love you because of your sincere honest heart, which reflects the love God has granted you! We want to continue praying that what God has started, sustained and deepened in our hearts will continue to grow by His grace and leading. We need Him as our counselor, source, adviser in all future decisions and plans! We want to continue trusting in His healing power despite all human facts. His potential remains unrestricted despite Satan's attempts to destroy...

...being strengthened with all power according to His glorious might so that you may have great endurance and patience, and joyfully giving thanks to the Father, who has qualified you to share in the inheritance of the saints in the Kingdom of lights. For he has rescued us from the dominion of darkness and brought us into the Kingdom of the son he loves. In whom we have redemption, the forgiveness of sins. (Col 1:11-14)

So feel like you have come home again! God will bless our future!

In love! Yours Martin

God was good to us as we settled into a daily routine. I lived in a nice apartment that DIGUNA had organized for me with a kitchen and sitting room for us when we had guests or wanted to be alone. Martin continued to sleep in his room in the men's quarters at the DIGUNA station. In the morning I went to German school and every afternoon around four o'clock we went for our afternoon walks. This was the best time of the day for both of us. It was spring and we had many days where we walked for two hours in the afternoon and Martin had no pain in this time. Some of the time the doctor would phone and enquire how Martin was and our DIGUNA friends would tell him: "he is out for an afternoon walk with his fiancé." The doctor could not believe that this was possible with the amount of cancer that was in his body. Many people were praying for us and I believe their prayers were answered in that he had no pain.

In these days we also planned our wedding. When we walked to the "Standesampt" (Town Court) in Haiger we met with Herr Gail. He was very kind to both of us and understood our situation. He checked through all my documents and we signed and filled out applications for our marriage. But there was one document that the German law still required. Most foreign countries cannot provide this document and Herr Gail wrote a request to the main Frankfurt court to find out if we could get legally married without this document. This we were told could take about two weeks. God again had His favour upon us and in His power organized it for us in just five days! Martin received the confirmation in the post that we could get legally married without this document. It was the Monday just before Easter and he phoned Herr Gail to find out when we could make an appointment to see him to arrange our marriage. Herr Gail said he had 10am the next morning free for us and that he would be happy to marry us! Martin said yes he would like that and confirmed the appointment. Then looked at me with a big smile on his face and said: "We are getting married tomorrow!" (the 7th April 2009)

Thankfully Martin's parents were with us as we had just spent the weekend with the whole Bezold family for Martin's niece, Helena's confirmation, and we had driven back to Haiger together. We had waited and prayed for so long and now suddenly we were getting married the next day! Martin phoned his church elders to let them know the news while his dad took me down to the local flower-shop to order some flowers for our big day. They would only be ready for me to pick up the next day just before our wedding. I had learnt that you normally do not wear your wedding dress to the "Standesampt" wedding, so I planned to wear a simple red dress that I had had for years. I had my black BATA sandals from Kenya and one of the ladies working at DIGUNA made me some pearl-like earrings and offered to do my hair in the morning. I had no time to plan any major details but it all felt wonderfully spontaneous and cost us nothing! Many of our friends in DIGUNA asked if they could come. Jo asked if he could be our photographer and so in no time at all everything was organized. We walked to the "Standesampt" and picked up the flowers on the way with our DIGUNA friends walking with us. When we arrived we were happily surprised to see Martin's church elders and their wives at the "Standesampt"; they had taken the day off especially for our wedding! Herr Gail asked Martin if there was anything special he wanted in the ceremony and he asked if the ceremony could end in prayer by Thomas the elder from his church. Corinna my good friend from DIGUNA translated the ceremony for me. Herr Gail even included a part of the South African National Anthem in English and it really touched my heart. It was the first time he had married a German and a South African so it was very special for him too. After we had signed all the official documents, Thomas prayed and then Herr Gail said to Martin: "You may now kiss your wife, congratulations Herr und Frau Bezold!" We were both so gloriously happy. As we walked out of the "Standesampt" the rest of our DIGUNA friends were all there and played and sang a beautiful German song and blessing; it was a wonderful spring day. We all walked back to the DIGUNA base and I felt such incredible joy and thankfulness to God. As we came around the corned to our base I was again surprised to see beautifully laid out tables and chairs like a garden restaurant, all ready to continue our wedding celebrations. The whole day was such a joy and I had planned and done nothing, except to sign the register making my marriage to Martin legal in the eyes of the German government.

We had both agreed that we wanted to have a church marriage ceremony before God before moving in and sleeping together in one room. This was hard for many people to understand but we both felt very strongly about this. Normally people would plan their church wedding a day or two after the official court wedding. However, we wanted to have my parents and grandmother from South Africa at our church wedding and had to wait for them to get their visas. Thus we planned our church wedding for the 2nd May. I had my white wedding- dress and white shoes ready and our church had planned to have a meeting to plan the decorations on the 20th April.

But God had a different plan for us on the 20th April. On this day, Martin's breathing had become so bad that he could not sleep at all; he also battled to eat and swallow his tablets. This was the first time I had seen Martin in a lot of pain. Our friends in DIGUNA had helped me move Martin to my apartment so I could look after him better and we had also organized an oxygen machine. But nothing was helping him. I realized in this moment that I could not manage to help him at all and we needed to bring him to the hospital where they could help give him pain-killers through a drip to ease the pain and give him some relief. When we arrived at the Wetzlar hospital the doctor told me it was the end and that we needed to say our last words before they injected Martin with Morphine. At that point Martin realized that I was going to faint and tried to tell them and I managed to find a chair and put my head between my legs. Then I managed to get some strength and came to his bed, he took my head and laid it on his lap and stroked my hair. He remembered that I had said long ago that when I was small and needed comforting my mother would hold me and stroke my hair. I looked at him with tears in my eyes amazed that he was still looking after my needs when he was about to die. He looked into my eyes and said; "Cath, will you forgive me for giving you such a hard time in Germany?" I told him that it was not his fault, that it was the cancer. He replied: "Cath, please look into my eyes and tell me you forgive me." In this moment I realized that Jesus was planning a much better and bigger wedding-feast for Martin in heaven and it was important for me to look into his eyes and forgive him and he spoke through all the things where he felt he had failed me and wanted my forgiveness. He knew how much I loved flowers and even asked for forgiveness that he had failed to bring me flowers. Of course I told him each time I forgave him and loved him very much. We then said the Lord's Prayer together. After overhearing us, one of the doctors came to us and exclaimed, "You are Christians!". One could see that she knew that the situation was no longer hopeless, she too knew where Martin was headed that day, and it was to a much better place. The hospital gave us a room to ourselves and I took three glasses and filled them with water. Then I said to Corinna and Martin that this was a celebration time before Martin went to be with our Lord in heaven. We then all clicked our glasses and said "prost!" (In English this means Cheers!) The next hour we spent singing worship songs and reading Scriptures. Martin was now on Morphine but he was worshipping with us and it was just wonderful. Corinna then left and returned to Haiger.

This was our first night together side by side in bed. Martin was in much pain now, he had a high fever and was really battling to breath so I just stayed with him and wiped his forehead, trying to keep him as comfortable as possible. Then at 3am in the morning he grabbed my hand and said; "Cath ich liebe dich so sehr."(I love you so much)", and I said: "Martin mein Schatz ich liebe dich auch so sehr."(Martin, my darling I love you too, very much)

In the morning Martin was sleeping. His parents arrived and together we stayed around his bed with Corinna and our pastor. When I held his hand I realized that there was no more feeling in his hand and prayed and asked God where I could hold him that he would know I was still there. I felt led to hold his head and in this moment I sang "Amazing Grace." Martin then opened his eyes and looked at us. I had promised him that I would be with him and would hold him until Jesus took his hand. I really saw how true it is in Psalm 23 where God says that when we walk through the valley of death He will be with us. Martin was so peaceful and did not fight death. Every time I had given him a sip of water during the day, he would thank me, but later on he began saying, "Thank you, Jesus", instead of "Thank you, Cath". I really felt like he was speaking directly to Jesus at that time and it felt as if Jesus was really there with him. After I had sung "Amazing Grace," Corinna read a scripture and as she finished he went peacefully into the arms of Jesus. I let his head go and Corinna held me as I wept. He was an incredible friend, fiancé and husband and I was proud to have been his wife even if it was only for two weeks.

My family eventually arrived but for a funeral instead of a wedding. We had Martin's funeral and then on the 2nd May both the Bezold family and the Fitzpatrick family went with me up "Signalstein" where Martin had proposed to me. When we got to the top I threw some flowers off the top in memory of our time and in memory of Martin. When everyone walked down my dad stayed behind and then held me in his arms as I wept and he prayed for me.

One evening my dad and I went for a long walk and I asked my dad how I was to move forward. He had given me over to Martin and I had walked through all the emotions of letting my dad go and now that Martin was gone I was not sure to whom I belonged anymore. My dad was quiet for a while and then took my hand and said: "Cath you are an eagle that flew from the home nest, and now your wing has been injured and you have again returned home under my wings until you have healed and can leave the nest when you feel ready". My dad was so wise and I just loved the way he responded to me, it comforted me to know that I was not a little eaglet again, but rather an eagle with an injured wing that needed time to heal. My family understood and supported me in my decision to remain in Germany for at least a year to complete my German school and spend time with Martin's friends, family and church.

I learnt in those days, weeks and months to be honest about my feelings and emotions. I learnt to feel free to cry whenever I needed and allowed my friends to comfort me. I can remember in this time reading many of the letters that Martin had written to me in the years that we had shared together. I started from the beginning when he first wrote to me and I was amazed to read it again:

"So far for now I would like to share with you 3 words from our Father which were comforting and directing me during the last days:
1) Isaiah 43:19a:"Behold I do a new thing...now it shall spring forth."
2) Psalm 37:4; "delight yourself in the Lord, and He shall give you the desires of your heart."
3) Hosea 6:1-3; "Come let us return to the Lord, for He has torn, but he will heal us, He has stricken, but he will bind us up. After 2 days he will revive us. On the 3rd day He will raise us up, that we may live in His sight. Let us know, let us pursue the knowledge of the Lord. Yours Martin"

God already told us in the beginning through his Word what would happen. Firstly, from Isaiah that something new would spring forth. Our relationship had blossomed into a beautiful flower and certainly did open up into a beautiful flower on our wedding day and we could with surety see what God had done for us. He had also given the desires of our hearts that we could get married and be together. Then thirdly, Martin had returned to our Lord, death had torn Martin and I apart and in Hosea it promises that He will heal and bind us up. This I held onto that Jesus would heal me, hold me and bind up my broken heart. In the days after Martin had passed away, I went for walks alone and I would talk to Martin as if he was there with me and tell him about the beautiful flowers I saw and

I would read his letters as if he had just sent them to me. But after reading the above Scriptures I realized that the life we had was no longer; it took time for that to sink deep within my heart. I decided that it was better for me when I went for walks, to talk to Jesus about the flowers and I read His Word more and more instead of Martin's letters to me. I really experienced how alive God's Word is and how it ministers to the heart and mind, brings comfort and love. In this year of healing God really provided all my needs, provided amazing new friends. I learnt to smile and even laugh again.

One thing I was afraid to do was to hope again for my future. I had prayed for so long to be married and have a family of my own and this dream had been snatched out of my hands. But I was determined to believe that God was painting a bigger picture for His glory out of my pain. I wanted to praise Him through it. I never seemed to have the question "Why, God?" But rather, "How, God?" How can I get up in the morning, how can I moved forward? God did show me how – through Him. My strength, my love, my faith and hope grew each day.

It is now the 1st May 2011 as I write this chapter and when people ask me if I wish I could turn the clock back, I can honestly say that I don't. Firstly, because I know Martin is free from cancer and very happy in heaven and I would never want to pull him away from such a glorious place. Secondly, I have seen how what I have been through has opened so many hearts to think about their lives in the context of eternity. Martin and I were willing to go to Sudan to share the hope we had in a relationship with God through Jesus Christ. Martin's death became that seed that has grown into a heavenly flower that we will only see in its full glory in heaven. Thirdly, I have been able to hope and pray again for God's plans for me and I still believe his promises for me to be married and have a family.

Martin's parents phoned me a year after Martin's death and they said to me on the phone that they wanted me to be happy. I told them that I was, and then Martin's dad said: " What we are trying to say is we want you to get married again." I was stunned and amazed, their love for me amazed me. I then phoned my dad and he said that he felt I had now been released and given the freedom to hope and pray to get married again. I must be honest I was not completely ready at that time. But over time I was able to truly hope and pray with my friends for God to lead a man into my life, a man that loves Jesus and wants to follow Him as I do.

Many people told me I should write a book about my life, others told me to wait until the story got better. But I felt led by God to write it now because I feel that many of us in our journey through life have dreams that have been taken away. I want to dream and hope with you for your dreams, as I pray and hope you pray with me for mine.

But while we wait on the Lord to answer our prayers, we should use the time for Him and for His glory. Our singleness or widowhood can be used for Him. So let us seize the day! Let us run the race that is set before us and throw everything off around us that is stopping us from moving forward in Jesus Christ.

In the year that Martin died(2009) I decided to continue German school and complete the requirements of the German Embassy. I had to go to school everyday until I had completed 600 hours of German school and three exams including a historical and political exam in German. In the beginning school was very challenging but I saw how God used it to help me get up in the morning as I did not want to face each day after Martin died. It also helped me communicate a lot better with the Bezold Family and my new found friends in Germany. Towards the end of the year I was able to share my testimony and the Sudan work in many churches around Germany and was able to do it without translation and in German!

Last year I returned to South Sudan and continued the work that we had started. I am now starting a new project in the village Ohilang where Martin and I had planned to work together. I still feel called to bring God's love and Word to them. I continue to work with the mission that Martin was with – DIGUNA - and they have been a great support to me. My friends and supporters in South Africa and now Germany, England, America and other parts of the world have touched my life deeply and supported me as I have followed Jesus in this calling. If you have bought this book or received it as a gift then you too have contributed to the ministry and work in Ohilang.

So my dearest reader, my prayer is that this book has built your faith to hold onto Jesus no matter how deep the valley is and that you too can dream and hope again in the plans Jesus has for you, just as I have been able to do again.

ABOUT THE AUTHOR

Catherine has been a full time missionary over the last 12 years of her life. She continued her missionary work in South Sudan. It was four years of being single again and a widow and then God brought someone into her life which has begun a new story and adventure. She is in the process of writing a sequel to this book.